A stoic recovery of disordered seasons

A stoic recovery of disordered seasons

Nicola Easthope

Cover image | Nicola Easthope

ISBN 9781763825970

Walleah Press
South Launceston
Tasmania, Australia 7249

www.walleahpress.com.au
ralph.wessman@walleahpress.com.au

Walleah Press

A stoic recovery of disordered seasons

Nicola Easthope

Contents

This poem was not written by AI

I remember the thundering, the air filled
with a gathering pace—hooves, tussock, volcanic dust.
The mountains cloaked for a moment as the plateau shuddered
with the muscle of horses. Streaks of colour like the flanks
of the Desert Road: chestnut, dark brown, dun, bay, strawberry roan.
Out of this herd sentience, a stallion
slowed and reared (of course he reared),
screamed. I remember the girl

in love with her mind, her pencils of graphite and pigment,
her pack of twelve for colouring in, baking paper cellotaped to the window.
A wildness formed as she traced him neat from a torn up magazine.
And she knew her horses—the points and shades of them, their gaits
and ailments, how to ride. Though there was no money for her own,
she had her lessons, she had her poem. *Mustang*. She tamed it real
and rode it bareback into class. With the force of horses in her trembling
body, she gave it to her teacher. A week later, it was returned—*Original?*
in red. There was no way to prove it and nothing more to be said.

Take away *I remember* and that's about as close
as I can get. There was the tearing to pieces,
the stuffing in the bin. My child, faceful
of thunder—tell your teacher—
saddle up, where do you think this is leading?

Stay in place

An aircraft shell passes over the house.
Rubbish trucks rattle the streets.
Two knives tink in the knife block.

I am circling my hips one hundred times
one way then the other—pelvic spells
with tea. Sip, circle, swallow.

A starling flies at the window, stalls
rump-facing, splats one on the pane.
Rejoins its chimney kin, whistling—

Window seat on the weathervane!
I have nothing to declare, nothing to bin,
just excess shit at the baggage reclaim.

Nonessential kiss

I thought we'd meet in Island Bay
on a park bench facing the wuthering sea.
Well, you two on it, in your safe bubble;
us three standing, two metres away.

There'd be coffee poured from the flask
steaming against the strait's new ice
and muffins with feijoa's soapsour grit.
We'd lift our masks, inhale.

I would swap this isolation for a chance
to slip on the mussel-kelp-anemone rock
so the soft creases of your cheeks
might catch my wishing lips.

Sweet FA but a dog's hunger

We are cleaning the house like it's for sale.
Even the twelve-year-old drops out of her world to scrub.
We are inhaling the internet like it's salt and vinegar.

Fog hunkers in the channel so we can't see the island.
We can't even see the neighbours two metres in front.
We sleep like long swollen lolling tongues.

I wonder how much of everything is real.
He shows me a clip of a woman dancing
with other women hard up against the deejay.

He marvels at her hands, such lovely fluent animals.
Well. I can do that, and show him.
No, he says, that's all spikey, like spiderlegs.

In the oncoming front that is our daughter's latest short story
there is horror and justice in simple violences of survival.
She laughs up a storm, in full control of her fictions

and goes off for a scoot, flying around the block.
After ten minutes, I see myself lurch
towards the landline.

At least my lockdown dreams are highly polished.
Tonight, I lean against a balcony without the rail.
Below, my middle-aged man cradles hands half his age.

Still life in an op shop

Dylan is sixteen and feels he's been working here
part time for too long. He's sorting reject CDs by genre
and thinking, this is such an old person thing, not retro
enough yet. Customers mull at the table of vintage crockery:
Temuka bowls and Crown Lynn, Arcoroc mugs, clear glass
with the embossed crocuses. Everybody wants to save nature now—

flowers on tea towels, mountains in frames. There's a box block
matt print like some DeviantArt they've chucked thinking
some sucker will love this! Dylan stares at it so long he wonders
if he can love this—flamingos flocking with a pink toothbrush
on a lean in a salt flat—the kind you see in Bolivia on the internet,
at altitude, in sunsets but without pop surrealist toothbrushes.

The boss is talking about the weather with one customer
after the other. What a mild winter we're having! Eighteen degrees
and sunshine in June! We are so blessed. Our summer sale rack is bare!
It's not good, really, thinks Dylan. The Greater flamingo depends on
rainfall to help it mate. See the flock's formed in a chevron
across the dry distance,
in hope. But the Even Greater toothbrush head is doing fine.
Let me carry it out

for you, he says to a girl with glitter tipped fingernails
shaped like long coffins.
Daylight stipples her face, there's a crackling in the air—
a crash, splash, shells, skeletons. Thank you, she smiles.
We really do live in
#paradise.

Though there are problems, today—you're really perfect

You walk the yellow trail of mid-morning.
No work for once, no weather presses in.
You take the keep cup filled at the coffee cart
remove the lid, blow the steam swirling
from the term, from the half-year, from all
that surreality has plagued and pleasured you with.
You see new colour in the gardens, follow the flowers
through the old tunnel of trees, cross miniature train tracks
to the beach where white-fronted terns
gather and drift at the ribbon mouth
of the Wharemauku stream. The window's
down in a car cruising past the brasserie
and the track they're playing takes you back
to Queen Street, mid-nineties, Emma Paki
at the Temple Cafe. You take the notes
of greenstone across the small bridge
to the north side where macrocarpas cling
into wind-buttered clay and their canopy shags
are out skimming the spume of cetacean blue.
There's a certain holy rhythm to your holiday
already—caffeine uncoiling, salt air unspooling,
memory music loosening the knots in your stride.
Your eyes cast to the island live with its heroes and histories,
green blush glows from marine reserve to summit,
Rangatira to Tūteremoana and Waiorua
and right around—a treasure
heaved from earth-shock, try pot, bird-kill and back
to kaitiaki safe-keeping. New afternoon sun plays its brilliants
on Rauoterangi channel; gannets plunge at kahawai.
And though it is July with the days layered up short—
like muscle cars too close behind,
like boiled woolscapes in thick framing
like an interrupted after-lunch nap—
you find yourself lengthening, shucking off clothes,
heady for the sea.

Without your glasses on, anyone watching dissolves.
If rose-tinted clouds can pass on the gossip of spring,
you can do this. Just in undies, the sea claws you in,
laps at you with a force that dares you to live.
You dunk and draw like an iced tea bag
free from its string.
Back on sand, you're no towel,
skin tight and all wonder at everything.

Some boys

Some boys pass you
on skateboards fractionally faster
than your smoking hot roller skates
so that you don't so much
eat their dust as slowly choke on it.

Some boys pass you by —
their heads in the clouds,
just not your cloud. You wish
for overcast skies and a little inciting
wind. Some boys pass their hands

over you without stopping
to ask Would you like me
to or would you like to pass?
Some boys are passable -
worth a date at a James Bond flick,

Coke and Snifters,
until you hear they think
you have a punky nose.
Some pash and pass us on
to their mates. Some pass

as boys who like girls,
kisses with butterfly wings.
They make the best friends
after they make sure it's safe
to come out. Some pass

away by their own hand,
the ones who used to grasp and release
frisbees to the spinning skies,
the brightest minds
in heavy passage. Some hand

you a free one—*be a passenger in my epic saga!*
a drop and dangle earring,
a diamanté choker at the throat.
Some pass you off for another, leaving your heart
pulsing in and out of consciousness, out

for the most part in cupid's vaulted ditch
also known as your dusky pink bedroom,
door shut, shadow side of the house.
Some pass on secrets not meant for you
to carry, on your own or in the company of fellow drama

kings and queens, titillated escalators, misfortunate
matchmakers, premature wedding planners.
You love and you love but
this time you roll
over and down
boy-less streets
serving dust twisters
at high speed.

Sweet nothings (three months in)

If you are the godwit fidgeting,
        I am sun-compass set to rivermouth.

If you are pneumatophore coming up for air,
        I am propagule carried by heat tides.

As you fish in saltmarsh and mudflat,
        I decay in gravel and sand.

You, aeolian grain down the stoss slope,
        I, fluvial upwelling at the slipface.

You might think you are the best time of year,
        but I am the stoic recovery of disordered seasons.

If you are the long-range forecast, it depends—
        I am either open-cell honeycomb cloud
                or cold front stalling at the edge of the bed.

Room temperature

Thank you for opening the beetroot jar
with your masculine advantage wrists.
The preserve of apple cider and spirit
vinegar pulls on the undulations
of my tongue. Slices swallow solo
down my throat, blanched, marinading.

I know I go through them
these large jars of golden sun but
sliced beetroot to me is as
liquorice and gingernuts are to you
and we are supporting small farms

over the seas. Carbon miles aside—you and me—
we make a red mess from the bench to the floor.
You still have the strength to twist the lid
and I still have the thirst.

Party goer

The best neighbours are those who invite but don't mind
if you don't come. They're just glad to know that you
know about the imminent onslaught of sound
and aren't bothered. From your deck, there's a sight line
into the next-door lounge where a television
is animatedly watched and addressed

by a woman in a peach cocktail dress.
She seems to be somehow out of her mind
and, through binos, you see she's watching Eurovision.
These could be your people! Many a time you
would sing along to *Telephone Line*
and softly rock to ELO's amniotic sound.

Yes, Jeff Lynne's doo-wahh-doo-lang is a sound
that takes you back to parties at the best addresses
in the worst places. A host once gave you some line
about helping him to make up his mind
about you
but you just couldn't envision

it—he clearly had double-vision
and you noted the mock cool in the sound
of his Harvey Wallbanger voice. The thing about you
is you pretend you never have anything fitting to dress
in but, like that Swiss watch ad tagline, success is a mind
game. After a Sloe gin or two, everyone loves an A-line

mini and the kohl you still line
your eyes with creates a swimming-at-night vision
for the men you could still keep in mind.
You recall the new wave wall of sound
you liked men to undress
you

to. Suddenly, you
hear people mingling by the washing line.
You squint through the fence to check the dress
code. There appears to be a familiar united vision:
hot pants, Mary Janes and mood rings! You make a *far out* sound,
quickly change your clothes—you've changed your mind!

Hey, you, good looking middle-ageing vision—
take a line, follow the sound
Ms Lurex gold wrap dress—go blow their minds.

silver eye

the tauhou bounces
on stem of yellow marigold —
a green arcing rod   bird heavy
enough to bend but not   to   break

at the top of the bounce   is a small ocean-facing craft
a half kiwifruit stuck by a nail
in the trellis   a golden row boat

          grounded at high tide

that the   wee bird
could've easily landed
by perching
on the thin brown rind

but no   it bounces
for its sweetness   and the flower head
smashes against the bow
          like a soft bottle of champagne.

Bodies of water

Right before the kayak flips on the Ōtaki, a memory of the harbour:
orange, lime, lemon vessels sidling up to each other,
bows pointing to a centre like floating petals,
synchronised swimmers. We move out again and one
sprints, the boat lifting across the deck of another. Then another
and another until we are a four-sided tangy fruit raft
three storeys high. A group gathers on the roof
of the Band Rotunda in the city bay. The two bravest
at the base are cry-laughing
until gasping. Until
they can cope no more—
well salted, we wet exit and screw roll.
We dry off and dress up,
fizz through the late night on Courtenay—
ginger wine and feasting from a Lazy Susan at the Shanghai.

Day river dreaming in frond and mist. I am not reading the water.
The rapid drags like a smoker—suck, coil, flick.
Stuck under at the base of a rock, white wall rushes
wherever I open: ears, eyes, mouth holding out.
My hands should be sliding around the cockpit coaming—
one yank at the spray skirt loop and she'll be free. No but no,
only flailing and knocking at the foam. Prayers for a bubble
and a chandelier column of light.

Two men take weeks from another continent
to reach and right the boat. Find a trout woman,
juiced and scalloped in the gulp. Soon slapped
and made sure.
Mosquitoes sign their lives in blood.
Dragonflies take the stern backwards
to a stone beach, soft wings and bowing rain.
Bodies of water lift and cup her. She speaks
of misted angels and the future
in which she sticks to the sea.

Rare

(i.m. Dad, 11.12.36 – 23.08.22)

On a rare evening
the sea's sun-flash sinks to green
like a sudden flatline without the machine.

Do you remember when you'd dance us
in daylight, one child buoyant
on each sea-skin slipper?

In each bedroom, you'd dusk us
Somewhere my love
to sleep.

Your lucky shoulders
one for each —
steady we go!

Now we are thrown
by the curve of
the horizon.

Through the house

You were laid in the makings of late spring—
the luck of bird urgency and weather.
Gentle, in senses relative to summer,
late, now merging with early seasons,
a desire line from nest to nectar, through the house.

I try my best. Move energy and matter every day,
some law of physics with what, in the moment,
feels like love. I mist the peace lilies
before the leaves dust and tip brown,
clean the windows twice a year before guests:

one going over on the inside,
twice on the out until the glass shimmers
like a surface of morning ocean and
gaps between branches of trees.
Your forebears came to the feeder

in winter and now, you hurry to arrive:
small, olive-sheen wings. Too fast,
you beat against the fatal tilt
of the only window unjammed, open
to the flash of watertight sun.

Breast twisted, white belly up
on the hot deck, eyes and beak venting—
I bring you water and soft gloves. Lay you
in the shade beneath green lemons.
In minutes, you kick out the end.

Here is your mother
singing with the force
of her making, a shrill
hope-call and feathers
fleet at the edge of the tree.

I spray and wipe your faint print
from the pane. My guests arrive, too hot
to dine indoors. They glance and gloss
at the bush-nestled view,
the comings and goings of small birds,

the plucky grey sea coming into land
with no note of window, just gin, ice and a slice
of awning shadow, of wing.

That storm was no Muse — you're just procrastinating

(i.m. Renée, 19.07.29 – 11.12.23)

I like to think the hailstones the size of rugby balls
pelting city streets and suburban decks this afternoon
is you, storm-clouding off, on your way, making sure
we don't forget to vote the bastards out next time.
Though you wouldn't fancy big rugby ball hail —
you'd say typewriter hail, library doors opening hail,
hail of rue seeds and their yellow heads come summer.
Your computer keyboard would take over my screen,
backspace rugby balls for scone dough —
that great mass on the tray before you score
it into pieces and bake it for the mourners.

This afternoon, you chased a plane north out of the slaty
typeset sky and wheeled gulls inland, over my garden.
You spared the golden gooseberries in their paper capes,
the early sunflowers. Anyway, you'd say, hang on a minute,
I would never pound gardens with hailstones that size
— that's a Facebook photo of mushed up balls of ice
staged for knee-jerk reactions. Don't be fooled! My word.
Now get on with what you were meant to be writing.
And you'd laugh like a thunder cloud melting.

All hail, Renée. All meteorite showers, auroras and stardust,
e te māreikura.

Notes and Acknowledgements

Ngā mihinui to the following homes and first outings for individual poems:

'This poem was not written by AI' was longlisted for the Monica Taylor Poetry Prize (2024), judged by Renee Liang.

'Stay in place', 'Non-essential kiss', and 'Sweet FA but a dog's hunger' were written in March 2020 in early Covid-19 lockdown days.

'Still life in an op shop' was Highly Commended in the Caselberg International Poetry Competition, 2024, judged by Rhian Gallagher.

'Though there are problems, today—you're really perfect' was a love commission for a variety show at Te Raukura ki Kāpiti in 2022.

'Some boys' was published as a Friday Poem on *The Spinoff*, thanks to editor and Poet Laureate, Chris Tse, on 21 June 2024, which happened to be my 56th birthday :)

'Sweet nothings (three months in)' was included in *Sweet Mammalian Issue 10*, edited by Rebecca Hawkes and Nikki-Lee Birdsley. I was able to give it a whirl at the launch as part of LitCrawl in Pōneke in November 2024.

'silver eye' and 'Rare' were published in Issue #45 of *Shot Glass Journal*, February 2025.

'That storm was no Muse—you're just procrastinating' was written for legendary playwright, poet, novelist and teacher, Renée (Ngāti Kahungunu), who passed away aged 92. I read it at her beautiful funeral. You can find more on this special wahine at https://gannetink.home.blog/2023/12/21/remembering-renee/

**

My heartfelt thanks to my family for their love and support, and for putting up with my quiet moods when all seems calm on the outside but sometimes, poetry is going off like a herd of elephants swimming in the waterhole of my head. Thanks to my Pākehā ancestors waiting patiently in the margins... some of these poems happened when I was supposed to be writing about them for my Master of Creative Writing. Love always to my dear father, who always believed in me and to Mum, who still does.

Thanks to Bridget O'Shannasey for the love commission; to Bryan Walpert and our poetry workshop course at Massey University; to Lynn Davidson (and fellow students) for the excellent and much needed Zoom poetry courses and workshops across the hemispheres, especially during lockdowns; and to Maria McMillan who also gave me encouragement and feedback on some of these poems. Ngā mihi arohanui to Hinemoana Baker for sharing her astute and generous expertise with a draft of this collection. Grateful thanks to Ralph Wessman for his long-time enthusiasm to help me bring this work to fruition through his smart and lovely publishing house, Walleah Press. And to Renée, for ever.